A Choreographer's Cartography

Acknowledgements

Thank you to Peepal Tree Press for taking the risk, for the real dedication to new writing and writers, and for all the hard work.

Acknowledgments are due to the following publications where earlier versions of poems from this collection have appeared: *Addicted to Brightness* (Long Lunch Press, 2006), *Poetry Scotland* (40), *Sable* (Fall 2006), *Daemon* (7 & 8), *Freedom Spring* (Waverly Books, 2005), *Acumen* (51) and *Kavya Bharati* (No. 16).

Atempause – a series of poems commissioned by the Austrian Cultural Institute, Battersea Arts Centre and Apples and Snakes (London) inspired by and in celebration of the music Johann Strauss and the waltz.

Pleasure Beach – commissioned by the Brighton Festival.

Stories fae da Shoormal – written as a result of a collaboration with Finnish filmmaker and artist, Lotta Petronella.

The title poem *A Choreographer's Cartography* was featured in a collaboration with multi-media artist Sean Clark.

Many thanks to Christopher Brown and Jeremy Poynting for their discerning editorial eye; Mary Blance, Lollie Graham, Andrew Graham and Christopher Brown for their kind guidance on the Shetland dialect; Hannah at Peepal Tree Press for a fantastic cover design; and the literature department at the Scottish Arts Council for much invaluable support.

Much love and thanks to my family: Mum, Honey, Kulraj, Koo, Navi and Chris; and my friends for pal-ship, creative kinship, intellectual nourishment, love and support: Dorothea, Vaishali, Lotta, Jaki, Sean and Magda; very special thanks to my spiritual siblings – Dodger and Sy.

and love^n *(where n tends to infinity)* for you my yarta

A Choreographer's Cartography

Raman Mundair

PEEPAL TREE

First published in Great Britain in 2007
Peepal Tree Press Ltd
17 King's Avenue
Leeds LS6 1QS
UK

ISBN 1 84523 051 5
ISBN 13: 978 1 84523 051 7

 Peepal Tree gratefully acknowledges Arts Council support

Contents

Vivace

Atempause

for my yarta
love^n
and
b.p,f.

60° North

You swallowed my tongue
left me *fantin*,
without voice,

Now I look
for my tongue
in other people's mouths.

Shetland Muse

(My Craft or Sullen Art)

Outside dark molasses
absorbs the last juice
from a misshapen tangerine
and pours thick across the vale.
The wind furious at being
ignored whips the ocean to a roar.

Soon, the gloaming begins
and something in my lower back
stirs and, later, something
lying beneath my skin moves
and my hand casts spells
that appear garbled on the page.

Throughout the night, the moon,
just out of reach, plays with the sheep –
hide and seek – their bustle torsos
a strange comfort in a landscape
void of trees. While most sleep,
my ink luminous marks magic true.

Foula

full
of you – my ears hear
    no other sound
through these walls – your damp
fingers reach me, paint me blue,
and your violence leaves
    the rough
smear of salt
    on my lips

Mareel

liquid
    twilight   sea
            song   sung

Simmer Dim

Simmer dim
          even-soul-song,
                    light lives

Aurora

Shimmying
Sonorous iridescence
Dark skies hum
while *mirrie dancers*
entertain

Sheep Hill, Fair Isle

I begin sheepishly.
      Feel with fingers,
attempt to *roo*

your softness taut
in struggle. I soothe
      with lullaby;

you settle. In no time
at all the shear's song
reveals your baby skin.

      You free yourself
of me. Hoof away. My fingers
lanolin soft with your memory.

South Nesting, Shetland

December darkness,
the comfort of bed
creeps closer as hours
contract – folding in sleep.
Snug – the sound of rain
lonely against the pane,
waiting to be let in.

Stories fae da Shoormal

Here. Hear da ice craack.
Be still. Wir forever
on da move. Dis rodd
gengs naewye, dis rodd
gengs aawye. Da onnly
thing daat truly flaows is da sea.

Da sea lonnlie, da sea,
da sea seduces, da sea,
da sea screms, da sea,
da sea senses, da sea,
da sea, da sea. In me drems

der a rodd; it gengs on
laang, laang – forever. Unlichted,
unshadowed, I canna see
mysel, bit I kyen, Ah'm dere. Un-alon,
awaash o me, awaash o midnicht
blue. Da skies waash ower me.

Da ice craacks, da Arctic tundra
shivers, readjusts hits spines,
sends secret messages idda dialect
tae hits nerve-endins in Shetlan.
Dir ley lines here
vibratin, crackin – electric.

Strange hoo far awa
memories come tae be – laek waves
laevin da shore.
      Wha wis da wumman?
      Wha wis da man?
We met idda shoormal.
Dee. Dee. Dee.
Du wis my fire
wance – my man
o' da waves. Du cam,
rested upo my shore.
I wis dy first
I wis dy harbour.
Bit my love, my selkie
man, du wis
    run agrund. Aach,
        siccan a sad thing for a sailor.
An noo my love, da sea
is my rodd, da rodd my sea.
I traivel on, traivel on, traivel
   on, for my love
wisna meant tae be.
     Da ocean,
    da waves,
   da shoormal –
  dis is noo my place,
my warmin space, my
  restin, my faimily.

3.

unidentified-unknown-unseen-unheard-unvoiced
unopened-unrecognisable-disappeared-silent
suppressed-lost-forgotten-stolen-unmemoried
stilled-haunted-unspoken-memory-still-past-mystery

Du doesna mind
Ah'm forgotten
I donnt exist
Du's med me inveesible

Dis is my mindin
Dis camera, my umbilical ee
Dis is my memory
Reliable, dis doesna lee

unidentified-unknown-unseen-unheard-unvoiced
unopened-unrecognisable-disappeared-silent
suppressed-lost-forgotten-stolen-unmemoried
stilled-haunted-unspoken-memory-still-past-mystery

4.

Here, you hae ta be waatchful.
Nordern lichts happen
when you're sleepin.
Whaals sail by,
oot a sicht ahint ferries, tankers.
Be ever alert,
meteor shooers cascade
ahint your back, whispers
echo alang Da Esplanade,
transparent lives – while da days
pass, markit be *Da Shetland Times*.

5

Dis toon is no big anoff fur dee
ta loss desel. Ta hadd dee
dis toon is no big anoff.
But hit's peerie enoff ta echo
aa dy past lives; scremmin
fae every coarner, remindin dee
du wis wance wan o' da promisin eens.
Du lassoed dy tongue
shaepit him intae a "sooth mooth"
an knapped desel raa,
dy lugs prunkit fir approval.
Du becam da wan
destined ta geng far.
Noo, riggit in black
lik a *Reservoir Dug*, du
veils desel in da English
wroucht, wry wit, while
aroond dee shadows
hing fae nooses.

60° North

liquid rage
breaks glassy reflection
crushing blue-green sea

sun-pennies float
glinting, winking – selkies flirt
I want to dive in

Sumburgh Head,
watching the waves waiting
for whales

luminous star
burns constant
covered or brazen

helios rays, light waves
nurture, destroy
life in balance

Hairst Mön Hamefir

Da hairst mön ripe
wi mylk oozes licht,
da road a runwye.

Da sowl soars
tae dy rhythm – dy mony naemes
a poyim, dy mony naemes

a sang: Eshaness, Clousta,
Burrastow, Scatness,
Virkie, Hjaaberg, Yell,

Muckle Roe, Ronas,
Fetlar, Foula – dy mony
naemes a poyim,

dy mony names a sang.
Du's lang and du's tin,
yit da rocks, faithful,

protect dee. Du's lang
an du's tin yit da sea's
dy mistress.

Dy mony naemes a poyim,
dy mony naemes a sang.
Birds divorce fae da sky,

betroth dee, an nest dir sang.
Da Haigrie, Da Bonxie,
Snaa Fool an Maalie,

Tammie Norie, Whaup an Peerie Maa.
Dy mony naemes a poyim,
Dy mony naemes a sang.

Da hairst mön ripe
wi mylk oozes licht,
da rodd a runwye.

Da sowl soars tae dy rhythm
Dy mony naemes
a poyim, dy mony naemes

a sang: Herrislea, Noostigirt,
Vementry, Vaasa,
Klingragetts, Freester, Stoorbra.

Du's lang an du's tin
bit dy wildness waakens me.
Du's lang an du's tin

bit dy speerrit soothes.
Dy mony naemes
a prayer, a poyim

tae sea an lift, a sang,
fou o love-licht.
Dy mony naemes

a sang. Da
hairst mön ripe
wi mylk oozes licht.

Terra Infirma

Blood Season
(Week beginning 18th March 2003)

1

This night haunts
time strains the flow,
taut minutes stress,
snap this brittle day before
the blood comes.
   The taste of iron.
the shriek of empty space –

Tomorrow vibrates
the distance:
         a steel tsunami.

All hail
this international sport.
Sit back, watch the players –
wide-screen death live
from the safety of your home.

Witness
   the blood
      season begin.

Bald-eagles circle
under a hexagon of stars,
the olive branch long forgotten
over the years; 13 arrows
and more have arched
in deadly flight. Who now
will strip this blind might?
Annuit coeptis protects
and serves The White
House. Allies buzz, barter
in the big white hive.
Bittersweet honey aids pledges
of allegiance to the blood
trade. Discount brothers-
in-arms take the fatal sting
for black gold.

3

By mid-morning they have begun.
My head free-falling with the rolling
news, trying to make sense,
but feeling sick at heart, wrung out.
Stretched beyond wear, hope
                        hung out to dry.

4

Today, the children
left their desks
and asked questions

outside in the streets,
their mouths open,
their voices strong

5

And now,
for our viewing
pleasure, music
to segue CNN pictures
        of death
in slow motion

6

The Oscars,
America's finest,
careful, glistening,
in 'shock and awe'
at the surprising results.

Piercing Flesh

for Abas Amini and Shahin Protofeb

"I sewed my eyes so others could see, I sewed my ears so others could hear,
I sewed my mouth to give others a voice." Abas Amini, 2003

With your eyes sewn shut what dreams
       did you dream?
Was your freedom to be, unquestioned?
And with your ears sewn shut, what sound is
                    freedom?
What tone and timbre does it take,
       and whose voice carries it?
And with your mouth sewn shut
             what a song
you sang, what a poem
       to pin back deaf ears – what a noise,
what a cacophony,
and what a silence
to greet it.

Detox

I am addicted to your fingertips'
touch, a gentle tap across *querty*
words I read too much

into; I can't help but reply,
press my desire
into send. Don't care

about your 'circumstance',
I've no patience for timing;
I'm wired, hungry, rash.

Where is your sense
of sisterhood? You teased
that night we kissed

and danced, your beer
a diminishing hourglass,
while your hands advanced

down my naked back –
me, an inebriated Cinderella
in need of a detox.

If I could, I would
dive into the infinite web,
retrieve the message before

it settles in your in-tray,
go cold turkey and stop
this wait, the constant

check, the need
for instant gratification
that punches through

my day, incomplete
without the punctuation
of your presence.

Stepmother

Overnight I become
a child
      -less mother.

As quick as you
came, you are taken,
the gift of you gone

and I am less,
feeling more than
ever. We

were not consulted.
Just told. And I hear
that I am

no longer your mother,
no umbilical cord
no blood ties,

no rights.
I am not your mother,
but you are my son.

You chose me and I
chose you. We
are connected

across the Atlantic,
through the memory
of the sea. You

– my unexpected wedding
gift – pure love, delight, sunshine,
laughter and cheek.

Now   I   am
                              not   your
                                             mother
            mother
                        no
                                    more

mourn

                  o

                              mother
            mourn

                                                amour
            another
                                    mother
                                                            o
                  Step

                              Awa y

            Mother
                                          child
                                                -less

                                                      Mother
Step
                        away
                                    Mother
                  silent

Spither

Mythic mother, you diminish
feelings to fairy tales,
your tongue weaves webs.

Spiderwoman, I am caught,
I can not unspin this
infinite fable. Mother,

marooned in this place
of sleep, you chew my dreams
and spit saliva trails,

a silver sliver of apron strings
I can not cut and I am bound
to follow. Like mother, like daughter.

For M

Time is artificial, plastic
false – something we create
        to wrap around ourselves
and slowly suffocate. Downstairs,
she totters on four fragile legs,
so weak they barely hold her weight.

My quiet optimism begins
to buckle. A vein
throbs at the side of my eye.
From my desk, the view
changes overnight. A house
built in a day. Every piece,

every part, accounted for. Everything
created by working hands.
                        In this cold
Winter, something new, stone-strong
grew, while time leaked through my fingers.
The decision hangs silent in the air.

She looks at me, all equanimity, pure
love. The knowing passes between us.
Her paw outstretched, gold velvet
in my palm. I cannot bring myself
to make the call and the hours blossom
silently into precious, given days.

Cassen Awa

Exhausted, tender, cradle
head in hands. Dry
scalp offers snow,
fingers comb
      feathers
      of hair fall
something leaves
offerings to the thin day
baptized with tears.

Vivace

Pleasure Beach

Suze and I go way back,
been best mates since
our first day at St Margaret's.

I was there when her first blood
came. She saw me through
the humiliation of being picked

last for games. We stuck
to each other like glue.
People used to say *Are you two*

Lesbos? We'd fix them
with a look. Yeah, we
were tight – her and I

would egg each other on.
One time we skived and nicked
£300 quids worth of gear

from Ms Selfridge. It was a laugh!
Crammed together in the changing
room. Stuffing the gear

down each other's pants.
Suze made out she was pregnant
and wombled her way out.

We ran all the way back
to hers. And then gave each other
a fashion show. Yeah, it was all right.

After school,
didn't see her much, maybe
one night a week.

Then I don't see her for ages.
No texts, no nothing.
It was summer,

the holidays, and the days went
on forever like homework.
And then she texts *i'v met sum 1*

Steve. Steve takes Suze's cherry
round the back of Echo's –
the theme tune to the Titanic

was playing. Suze says that's their song.
I say nothing, just sink my eyes
into her purpleblue lovebite.

I know it won't last long.
She says they're at it every night.
That's when Bob comes

on the scene. He used to hang
around the schoolgates in his car
offering us girls lifts.

He was alright, a bit old but
nice. Saw him at the club
and he offered to buy us

drinks. We didn't say no.
Turns out he's got new wheels
and do we want to go out for a spin?

So next weekend we take off.
Me and Bob in the front
with Suze surgically attached to Steve

in the back. Hit the pedal and flew.
Ended up in Blackpool,
getting pissed on the Pleasure Beach

and chucking chips at biddies
in deckchairs, slurping
their packed lunch. It was alright for a bit

then Suze says she wants to ride
the ghost train. We jump the queue.
Inside, Bob's hands are like a rash:

all over me. It's a nightmare.
Suze snogs Steve, so I give in
and let him. He kisses like a frog,

makes me want to puke. His skin
luke warm and rough against my cheek,
he whispers *Rita Kuuu-maaar*

you taste of curry and spice.
Is that what my little girl's made of?
I can't breathe. We're at the end

of the tunnel. I rush outside
fighting for air. *Oi! What's your hurry?*
Suze catches up with me;

I throw up. Suze takes one look
at my face and says we need some girly
R+R, tells the boys to take off

and meet us back at the B&B
in a coupla hours. I don't know how
she does it: stays completely in charge.

Bob and Steve look at each other, shrug
and make for the bar. Suze takes me
by the hand through the sea of coconut shies,

waltzers, dodgems and camel jockey rides. I'm on
a roller coaster – my heart and stomach
don't know what to do. She stops and buys

two sticks of rock, with our names written all the way
through. *This'll sort your belly out* she says
and I take a stick and suck on 'Suze'. I'm feeling lucky,

steer Suze into the Penny Arcade
feed the hungry slot machines
like they're wailing babes,

stand mesmerised by the touch
of silver against silver in the shuffling
step machines, good fortune, just a hair's breadth

away. We angle the coins in like physicists,
hold our breath, wait for the sound
of a silver cascade. 'Til Suze slams

the glass, and breaks the spell.
We get booted out.
Bastard! screams Suze

Show me the money! and we leg it.
I ram her onto the tram. The oil slick
quiffs of sea wave in salute

as we whir our way towards our B&B.
Inside we crash, sprawl ourselves
across the bed and flick on the TV.

Do you think they still do it?
asks Suze eyeing up 'Richard and Judy'
Nah man! Would you? with 'im?

More like how does he with 'er?
Nasty! We near piss ourselves
laughing. It's like old times, me and Suze

just hangin'. Me and Suze close.
Me and Suze in our own world.
Interconnected, like the sea

and the shore. Suze stretches
out her legs and says her
bikini needs a bit of a tidy,

hands me the wax strips
lies back and waits. I ask her if she fancies
the full monty or a Brazil.

She goes for the landing strip.
I smooth down the wax
slowly, firmly and then rip at will.

She comes up smooth,
with a red, raw glow,
lights a fag and turns over.

I'm creaming up
watching Suze.
Her phone rings. I jump.

Steve and Bob are on;
Are yous coming or what?
Outside, light is fading fast

and the promenade is buzzing
with 'french-me-frank' hen parties
and 'kiss-me-kate' stags.

Suddenly someone flicks a switch
and the streets become magically lit.
Fluorescent and neon icing hangs

in the air. The tower pulsates
with electric juice and the taste
of fried fish and chips floats

past in newspaper cones. And the theme
park, a mass of illuminated
spaghetti is being devoured by the night.

We get to *Martinis*, the music is pumping,
the place is heaving and Steve
and Bob are wasted, propping up the bar.

Suze demands drinks and drags me
onto the dance floor. She spins
and gets into the groove.

She's knows all the songs,
and mouths the words, dancing
rings around me.

Steve staggers and grabs her hips
trying to gyrate. Suze looks at me
and pulls a face, breaks free,

slides over and holds me
in an embrace. We're dancing,
eye to eye, body to body

I'm in a candy floss dream;
I'm one of Cyndi's girls
just wanting *to have fun*,

and the way you hold me
makes me feel like
I'm the only one and I'm

Madonna's virgin
shiney and new – *touched
for the very 1ˢᵗ time*,

feeling so alive
all because I'm noticed
by you.

Steve slimes over and sandwiches
Suze. I'm trapped
in a *Sunday Sport* pose.

I try to pull Suze
away to the loo.
She's not having any of it.

I watch her shake her tits
Steve starts to salivate;
I want to punch his face.

I walk away
and take refuge in the loo.
Lock myself in

and slip my knickers off.
I'm creamed, wet, moist,
I stick my finger in

and sniff the sweet funk,
lick my fingers, squeeze my legs
and fantasize about Suze.

I come out
knowing exactly what I should do.
As I walk across

the dancefloor, couples part.
I pull Suze to me
and give her a good hard snog.

I don't hear anything
but the sound of her heart
I don't smell anything

but the heat of her funk
I don't taste anything
but the rightness of this love

and I don't touch anything,
but an angel in a woman's form.
and I don't see what's coming

and I don't see what's coming
You dirty girl Steve smirks
pulling us apart. *Just couldn't wait...*

She's well up for it, aren't you babe?
Suze smiles. I don't get it.
I watch her lips move

but she's speaking another language.
Me and you and him together
yeah? A bit of fun like.

My head feels punch-drunk
and I can't get out fast enough.
My stomach's turning, I spew

out onto the streets, into the fag end
of the night and my love
lies in ashes, and on my lips

the taste of her kiss mixed
with sea salt and the sobering
sour of vinegar truth.

Around me the sound of the great fruit
machine in the sky, as life blows me
three giant raspberries in a row.

Claritas

Meeting you, pure joy
  life makes sense
     – to be with you forever

Mirl

Wear the moon
Clutch it to your heart
Shimmer, shine

'Club Kali'

(The Dome, Tuffnel Park, London)

Liquid lights strobe
E'd up, keyed up
fade to loved up

    We spin, spin
    the laser romance.
    Tonight. The thump,

        the drum
           skin stretched across
        skin. Together we vibrate.

           Let me pulsate
           against your skin,
           feel my blood rush

                my heart pumps
                  me closer to you
                neon love licks

                    this our song
                    let the music
                    play on, play on...

Dizzy

Your fingertips paint me
I bend, flow
to meet your kiss

the marrying of mouths;
in your eyes,
a fire burns

nipple to lip,
suck, lick, kiss
don't stop now

and now blow me
like Dizzy Gillespie
soft, hard, strong, and long.

Gently, firmly, work
me until I melt.
I am yours.

Do not stop, come
with me, deeper, deeper.
We will swim.

The Morning After

Awake at 6, a sweet taste
in my mouth and full
of poems. The train
to Greenock: every tree
       reached out
to stroke my face.

A Choreographer's Cartography

These are not tentative steps
on terra infirma, this woman
feels the ground beneath

her feet. Read this
as a new dance.
Improvise – find free

ways to flow, stretch and claim terrain,
inhabit all regions of your body,
set forth and stride with natural grace.

Mark this ascent
in 16-beat time: *Ek, do, teen,*
char, panch, che, satt, ath,

no, dus, gyarh, barah, terra,
chaudah, pandrah, sola
– solar rhythms spin,

disrupt tectonic plates. Rethink,
re-scale, re-form, re-shape
cultural boundaries to create

physiques full with emotional geography.
You need no passport for pliant limbs
loose with joy. No visa,

no nationality needed for loving
kindness; claim your right for asylum
here – this earth – everyone's sanctuary.

Read this as a new dance
part of a loquacious movement
that hip-hops and celebrates border crossings

with bodies that boogie with belonging,
tap dance this tenacious topography.
You are here

raise your flag, feel the funk
get into the groove,
and pogo like a punk.

Lilt and sway with the reggae chill,
waltz around the world, re-orientate
with the thrill of a highland reel,

do the two-step, fox trot, twist and twirl;
this is a choreographer's cartography
a seductive salsa, this earth,

everyone's sanctuary;
fandango this formation,
take a partner, tango, do-si-do,

grapevine, calypso
merengue, bhangra, danzon
breakdance, bulerias and disco.

These are not tentative steps
on terra infirma, this woman
feels the ground beneath

her feet. Read this as new dance:
a choreographer's cartography –
this earth, everyone's sanctuary.

Atempause

Volvere

(A Historical Spin on the Waltz)

Strauß' quivering preludes ensnare the senses...

An immutable movement satisfied
    in itself; a couple replete
in wanderlust creating a dream

on tippy toes; a circular chase
like a dog after it's own tail.
Breast to breast,

moving in triple time
to a lyrical cadence;
lost, in delicate undulation,

a swooping swoon,
a swain's sigh –
    a coming

together. An endearing
ecstasy, a fantastic finale –
the waltz, a display

of flesh, a veritable orgy.
Viennese high society spins
while Western Europe bruises,

tumbling towards an industrial age.
Vienna, nostalgic, returns to nature:
the waltz king's quivering preludes

stirs it up: Rousseau with the *Dreher, Weller,*
and *Schleifer* sets the ballroom alight,
a rhythmic revolution is spun;

a dance which both frees
and anchors the spirit in the night,
and hails a time of etiquette, of elegance,

when women were ladies,
and men were gentle
-men. The elite float free and fade

out the sounds of Russia,
where workers march
for justice, equality and bread,

throwing themselves
into a heady spin. Twirling
around their goldfish world –

a powder-puff ball
in a cigar and cold meats kind of place;
a subtle fruit punch for the ladies,

and thimble of the finest vodka for the gentlemen.
Later, empires crumble at the turn of a ballroom gown,
as blood filters through Vienna snow.

A Servant's Tale

Part I

The fabric of your adornment,
the spectacle you project, has travelled
from the hands of my sisters and brothers;
muslin, silks, cottons, organza
woven in the textile mills of Punjab,

lifebloodcolour oozed from the dyeghats
of Rajasthan to Bihar, the delicate
appliqué and faerie-fine embroidery,
born from the pittance-paid pain
of hardened hands in darkened corners.

You seemed overwhelmed by the splendour
we create, need helping hands
to fix you into place: so many stays
to be hooked and ribbons bowed
and a powder-puff of white dust

to take the shine off of your nose.
As you dance around in your finery,
we flit unnoticed, serving you endlessly.
But behind closed doors we take your dance
and posture and make something honest of it.

Dancing, lightly, as if on sand,
we begin a new choreography,
and before you issue your command,
we summon sure steps towards freedom,
and impress a new cartography.

Part II

Uray lattha iddha lagthay see jaisay pinjra vich see.
Her legs looked as if they were inside a cage.
Ahie meri Ma kendi hundi see
That's what my Ma used to say
kuro au bari kargh wali memsahib vastay kam kardi hundi see.
when she used to work for the memsahib in the big house.
Memsahib thay upper kapri pandi hundi see.
She used to dress the memsahib.
Mai ta bilkul yakeen nahi kardi see.
I didn't believe her.
Mera matlab, kaunsi ji aurat apni ap nu pinjra de wich bethi haungi?
I mean what sort of woman would put herself into a cage?
Phir mai apnay ap ay dekhiya.
Then I saw it with my own eyes.
Au sarri bani hui, fasihuey,
All laced up,
aur pinjra vich beti huey.
trapped, and sitting in a cage.
Jaisay au gaun valay chirya,
Like a singing bird,
magar ai chiri da gana ta khatum hai,
but this bird's song has finished.
Hun koi awaz nahi
She no longer has a voice.

Part III

My madam's ballroom was a glorious sight,
a magnificent creation turning,
spinning, flowing and growing
throughout the winter night.

Through the crack of the door
I fancied I saw silverfish
and magical bluebirds fly
across a water-lily pond.

Lotus blooms floating in a gentle breeze,
whilst flashes of rust orange
leak a gold that decants
in shadows of lilac whispers

spiced with a promise of midnight blue.
I spy: the trace of hearts bleeding
into muslin white as the Vienna snow.
Secrets woven into the memory of lace.

It is I who dress her,
It is I who know:
her every rotation reeks
desire, a roving want.

It is I who know,
It is I who saw
her face turn pale, cold to the touch
of her husband's wrinkled paw.

And now he licks his lips,
turns and flicks his eyes on her,
betrays a cuckold's passion
that cuts and marks and burns.

Sweat beads her brow.
In this glass heat she's fading fast.
My lady's pastel poise begins to melt,
and taffeta icing sours,

cream curdles, sugar turns to salt. I feel
her roughshod scorn of my sun-kissed hands
that braid and comb her colourless strands,
that encase her in her whalebone cage

whilst she rages that she 'must have'
her waspish waist. I oblige – pull tighter
on her corset, fancy the air escape
her mouth like smoke.

And now she spins
like the turn of *dhai* into *lassi*
but now *lal mirch* is added,
and madam flows a trail

of blood *jalebi*-patterned.
Unknown, a life slips away
and her marionette face contorts
and her body crumples

broken-stringed
into the hollow of her dress.
A hush, the sound of night
-time snow drifts across the room

– an illumination occurs,
a realisation of reputation lost
as the pastel combustion
veers out of sight.

And it is I who knew, it is I who knew
that my lady was never as fair or as fresh as dew.
And it would have mattered not a jot
had she not scorned my sun-kissed hands

though they delicately caressed her locks.
That night, the heat of her pearls
lie heavy in my hands.
As I undress her,

I admire myself in the glass;
her eyes are lowered.
My roasted almond hues
are iridescent, against her shroud-

white tones. My quiet
eyes, once timid,
for the first time now glow
bright and speak.

The Blue Danube
and Tales From the Vienna Woods

They say the Vienna woods whisper
to the Danube and command its flow.
Forever the deepest blue,

I swimmingly whisper to you,
Will you come back
and dive again into these waters?

Your piano hands
adjust my hair,
a fragile tinkering;

I am all askew.
House lights dim,
and I am caught

in a narrow spotlight's glare.
I watch your distant lips mouth
a meaning, and my head

prompts another story. Your fingers create
a turbulence I cannot weather down.
I was a child born into expectation;

I coax myself daily into the present –
I perform, but this yearning
hollows me out.

Come close, listen:
I am a cavernous seashell
waiting to resound,

an intense need.
I experience the world
as heat or non-heat. In summer

the air trembles around me
as my orbit decays towards your heart –
a sonorous star. I am

your artist's material; mark me,
make me, forever.
I move away from the light,

down the 'drink me' potion
to once more be small
enough to crawl beneath your skin.

Faithless, your heart pounds
and I am excreted through your pores,
a scentless sweat,

a silent disappearing.
You take off your shirt and wipe away
the dust that lingers across my keys.

You finger softly
a long-memoried melody,
I yield and offer

a bittersweet symphony.
Your fingers create a turbulence
I cannot weather down

and there you go again, playing
'The Blue Danube' followed by
'Tales From the Vienna Woods'.

Vicky and the Sikh

Movement One

Victoria, grey Queen of a blood-red imperial empire,
had a penchant for Sikh warrior men. Had a fine specimen
ordered from the 'orient', to stand watch as she lay in her bed

from where she liked to watch him,
erect, tall and proud, tresses tucked seductively
under the twist of a cloth crown.

When alone, her blue blood rising,
she begged him to let down his hair, unravel
and turn, his abundance creating a peacock spray in the air,

until, no longer able to contain herself,
Victoria gathered him in her arms
and took her humble Sikh for a waltz.

The Sikh, a fine fellow,
a distinguished Sardar, one Harminder Singh Sahib,
bemused by the ash lady's advances,
would try to bhangra his way out of her iron clasp.

But alas,
undeterred and riled-up, the stoic Queen
ardently continued her enthused advances.

The pious widow, a true lady of grit,
cloaked only in shades of black and gypsum grey,
(accessorized with tasteful touches of white lace)
was in her kingdom the epitome of God's grace.

Indeed Vicky was viewed as an infallible Regina,
by her loyal subjects, whose feelings
towards their Queen remained forever fervent.
Her self-control was greatly admired, as was her charitable toil,
and her epic mourning for her Albert was debated near and far,
and it stood to reason that her noble, shy, Sardar
be deemed the perfect companion for a woman born royal.

So Vicky took
to clandestine clutches,
waltzing Harminder Singh Sahib.
But it was not an easy task;
the man from Punjab –
the place of five sacred rivers –
moved to an unchaste
rhythm, fluid with grace
– most unbefitting to the 3/4
discipline of the waltz.

After much coaching
and coaxing Victoria
was almost at the end
of her royal tether
as her warrior man
would synchronise
with a secret music
Her Highness
was unable to colonise.
The Singh held his distance,
thwarted V's unquenched desire
and the propinquity
essential to the waltz.
The Dance! Harry!
The Dance! Vicky
would hysterically shriek
as Harminder Singh Sahib,
sought his leave to retreat.

As a last ditch, desperate
measure, Victoria
decided to bind
them together
with a ball
of leather twine.
Both partners bound
in the rhythm
of 3/4 time.

Back straight! Back straight!
she bellowed in the Singh's delicate ear,
the poor fellow near crippled
by the old lady's weight,
as her bejewelled hand bore
down on his arousing gait.
She marched their bodies
into a burgeoning spin
Madam, please! Madam,
please! the Singh begins,
his patience at an absolute end.
But the old lady is for turning
and takes her captive man
for yet another spin
and orders *Again Harry!*
Again Harry! Again!

The Ghost Waltz

(Gueca Solo)

for Victor Jara

I

I try to become like the waves:
roll and wash away, but the debris
of myself clambers ashore.
My feet move independent
　　　of me. The day
you disappeared, my body
went AWOL. I am incomplete.

Time stills, in black and white,
your photograph pinned
across my heart. I dance
alone while the toy soldiers watch;
I swallow my screams.
I know my arms are empty,
but your spirit fills me

and I am dancing for your memory,
turning heavy circles,
trying to transform the grief,
into what we may not say. No
poppies red or white —
this is an invisible war,
where having a voice endangers.

Better to be mute
turn a negative
into proofs
that can be identified.
I am dancing your memory
　　　ghost waltzing,

churning away my fear,
spinning it into courage
and light, trying not to blur
my last image of you,
precious in my mind's eye.
Time
has cheated me.
Stolen.   My child
gone and I still cannot believe.
I dance alone
severed from within
and without you –
without you I am nothing.

II

One of many am I,
mourning for the vanished face
of a father, brother, lover, son;
a memory as vivid as a limb
amputated without anesthetic.
We dance, septic with loss.

It was the cruel conjuror's trick –
How could he have hidden you all?
Global eyes avert, create a vacuum
into which all sorts of atrocities crawl.
I hear Pinochet takes tea
with the Iron Lady, indulges
her fondness for expensive chocolates,

whilst he reclines behind the doors
of an exclusive Harley Street address.
They sip Earl Grey in Wedgewood
and spin sugar with silver spoons
and reminiscence, about hours spent
playing war-games at Number 10
and compare notes.

The Last Waltz

A heavy stringed intro,
a dress laced with a melancholic trim,
faltering steps in ill-fitting shoes.
I am not used to dancing backwards:
you lead, I follow, not
matching your surefootedness.

Let me be the one to say it:
Unbreak the charm,
recant the spell,
undrink the potion,
claw back the days.
We are out of time.

We come into life
reeling towards the last waltz
and with each revolution
I come closer, a whirling dervish:
ecstatic and blissful
in the not knowing.

Notes and Translations

'Stories from the Shoormal'

1.

Here. Hear the ice crack./Be still. We are constantly /on the move.
This road/goes nowhere, this road/goes everywhere. The only/thing
that truly flows is the sea.

The sea lonely, the sea,/the sea seduces, the sea, /the sea screams, the
sea,/the sea senses, the sea,/the sea, the sea. In my dreams

there is a road that continues on/long, long – forever. Unlit,/
unshadowed, I cannot see/myself but I am there-Un-alone,/awash of
me, awash of midnight/blue. The skies wash over me.

The ice cracks, the Artic tundra/shivers, readjusts its spines,/sends
secret messages in dialect/to its nerve-endings in Shetland./There
are ley lines here /vibrating, cracking – electric.

2.

Strange how far away/memories become – like waves/leaving the
shore/Who was that woman?/Who was that man?/We met at the
shoormal./You. You. You./You were my fire /Once, my man/of the
waves. You came,/rested upon my shores./I was your first
/I was your harbour./But my love, my selkie/Man, you were/run
aground. Ach,/ such a sad thing for a sailor. /And now my love the sea/
is my road, the road my sea./I travel on, travel on, travel/on, for my
love/was not meant to be./The ocean, /the waves, /the shoormal – /
this is now my place, /my warming space, my/resting, my family.

3.

unidentified-unknown-unseen-unheard-unvoiced/unopened-unrec-
ognisable-disappeared-silent/suppressed-lost-forgotten-stolen-
unmemoried//stilled-haunted-unspoken-memory-still-past-mystery

You do not remember/I am forgotten/I do not exist/You invisibilised
me

This is my memory/This camera, my umbilical eye/This is my
memory/ Reliable, this does not lie

unidentified-unknown-unseen-unheard-unvoiced/unopened-unrec-
ognisable-disappeared-silent/suppressed-lost-forgotten-stolen-
unmemoried/stilled-haunted-unspoken-memory-still-past-mystery

4.

Here, you have to be vigilant./Northern lights happen /when you're
sleeping./Whales sail by/hidden behind ferries, tankers./Remain
ever alert, /meteor showers cascade /behind your back, whispers /
echo along The Esplanade,/transparent lives – while the days /pass,
marked by *The Shetland Times*.

5.

This town isn't big enough for you/to lose yourself. This town isn't
big/enough to contain you. /But it's small enough to echo /all your
past lives; screaming /from every corner, reminding you /that you
were once one /of the promising ones. You/lassoed your tongue and
shaped/it into a 'south mouth'/and knapped yourself raw, /your ears
pricked/for approval. You became the one/destined to go far. /Now
dressed in black /like a *Reservoir Dog*, you /veil yourself in wrought,
wry/English wit, while shadows/ hang from nooses around you.

From title page '60° North', p.9.
fantin (Shetland dialect) – hungry, starving.

From 'Mareel', p. 13.
Mareel (Shetland dialect) – phosphorescence seen on the sea, especially during Autumn nights.

From 'Simmer Dim', p. 14.
Simmer dim (Shetland dialect) – long Shetland summer nights, when the sun barely sets.

From 'Aurora', p. 15.
mirrie dancers (Shetland dialect) – Northern Lights/Aurora Borealis.

From 'Sheep Hill, Fair Isle', p. 16.
roo (Shetland dialect) – to remove fleece by hand.

From 'Stories fae da Shoormal', pp. 18-22.
shoormal (Shetland dialect) – the place where the sea meets the shore.
sooth mooth – from 'sooth moother', Shetland slang for a person from mainland Britain; i.e., someone who has come to the South Mouth of Lerwick harbour on the ferry.
knapped – to *knap* is to speak English as opposed to dialect.
prunkit – ears cocked and alert like a sheepdog.
Da Shetland Times – the local island newspaper.

From 'Hairst Mön Hamefir', pp 24-25.
Hairst Mön (Shetland dialect) – Full, round, romantic, autumn moon.
Hamefir (Shetland dialect) – Homecoming.
mylk – milk.
licht – light.
runwye – runway.
sowl – soul.
naemes – names.
poyim – poem.
Eshaness etc. – places in the Shetland Islands.
lang – long.
tin – thin.
dee, du/dy – you/ yours.

lift – sky.
speerit – spirit.

From 'The Blood Season', pp. 29-31.
Annuit coeptis – Inscription on US currency. Taken from the Latin words annuo (to nod, approve) and coepio (to begin, undertake); a literal translation means someone or something 'favours the things having been begun'.

From 'Piercing Flesh', p. 32.
Dedicated to Abas Amini, Shahin Protefeh, Ali Mohammed and Azad Hazan
Abas Amini (an Iranian Kurdish political poet), Shahin Protofeh, Ali Mohammad and Azad Hazan all experienced torture in Iran and fear for their lives. They sought asylum in Europe (Azad Hazan was being held at Sangatte Refugee camp in Calais, France, the others in the UK). Their applications for asylum were refused and in protest at this decision, they sewed up their eyes, lips, and ears. At the time of writing this poem, only Abas Amini had been granted refugee status.

From 'Spither', p. 37.
spither (Middle English) – spider.

From 'Cassen Awa', p. 39
Cassen awa (Shetland dialect) – lost.

From 'Pleasure Beach', pp. 43-51.
biddies (English, colloquial) – old women.

From 'Mirl', p. 53
Mirl (Shetland dialect) – shimmer.

From 'A Choreographer's Cartography', pp. 57-58.
Eik, do...solah (Punjabi/Hindi/Urdu) – One, two ... sixteen.

From 'Volvere', pp. 61-62.
Volvere (A historical spin on the waltz) – In its origins, the waltz was a

revolutionary dance in many ways. For example, it was the first dance in Europe that permitted dance partners to be in close proximity. The poem traces its roots from its folk dance traditions to its philosophical and political connotations and impact upon Viennese high society.

From 'A Servant's Tale III', pp. 65-67.
Dhai into lassi (Panjabi/Hindi) – yogurt that is whisked into lassi, a refreshing drink.
Lal mirch – red pepper, added to lassi to make it savoury.
Jalebi – a delicate coiled sugar sweet in a vivid orange red.

From 'Vicky and the Sikh', pp. 70-73.
Bhangra – (Punjabi/Hindi) - A joyous North Indian folk dance.
Sardar – A Sikh man.

About the author

Raman Mundair is a writer and artist. In 2007 she was awarded an Arts Council England International Fellowship at the India International Centre in Delhi. She was runner up in the Penguin Decibel Prize for Short Fiction in 2006. As a playwright she was awarded a mentorship with the Playwrights Studio Scotland in 2005, where she worked with Peter Arnott. In 2006, she collaborated with the National Thetare Scotland Young Company on *Side Effects*, a one act play which went on to tour Glasgow, Edinburgh and Dublin. Her play, *The Algebra of Freedom*, will be produced by the award-winning 7:84 Theatre Company and open at Edinburgh Festival Fringe in 2007.

Raman's writing has been featured on BBC Radio 4's Women's Hour, BBC London, BBC Asian Network, and the BBC World Service; and has been used in teaching at The Open University, Florida International University, University of Aberystwyth, University of Portsmouth and Roehampton University.

Raman has been Writer in Residence in Stockholm, Oxford, Maidenhead, Slough, Glasgow and the Shetland Islands and has represented The British Council as a writer, workshop facilitator and performer internationally.

As an artist she makes work that represents text and narrative in a visual form. her work has been exhibited at the Gallery of Modern Art Glasgow, City Art Gallery, Leicester and The Generator Gallery, Loughborough.

Her debut collection of poems, *Lovers, Liars, Conjurors, and Thieves*, was published by Peepal Tree Press in 2003.

Also by Raman Mundair

Lovers, Liars, Conjurers and Thieves
ISBN: 1-900715-80-5; pp. 96; pub. 2003; Price: £7.99

From beginnings secreted in the folds of her mother's sari, transplanted to England to struggle with the rough musicality of Mancunian vowels, Raman Mundair, a Punjabi Alice, found no true reflection of herself, no wonderland, but mirrors which dissolved, shrank and obscured her size. In these poems she creates her own universe and dissects its realities in all their complex, tragic and surreal forms.

At the heart of the collection is an acute sensitivity to the body: hurt, aroused, desired, ignored. Her poems spill out from this centre: to the physical memory of domestic violence, the intense joys of intimacy and love, and the pain of their rejection, to a passionate concern with the body politic. Here the approach is oblique, metaphorical, observant of the details that carry the poems beyond political statement.

"She is constantly sensual... tempered by a delicate care for detail, a quality of consideration that engages in the philosophical in sometimes complex ways..."

– Kwame Dawes

Other related titles

Seni Seneviratne, *Wild Cinnamon & Winter Skin*
ISBN 13: 9781 84523 050 0; pub., 2007; pp. 64; £7.99

Seni Seneviratne's debut collection offers a poetic landscape that echoes themes of migration, family, love and loss and reflects her personal journey as a woman of Sri Lankan and English heritage.
  The poems cross oceans and centuries. In 'Cinnamon Roots' Seni Seneviratne travels from colonial Britain to Ceylon in the 15th century and back to Yorkshire in the 20th Century; in 'A Wider View' time collapses and carries her from a 21st century Leeds back to the flax mills of the 19th century; poems like 'Grandad's Insulin', based on childhood memories, place her in 1950's Yorkshire but echo links with her Sri Lankan heritage.

'There's something about us. There are historians that may record our experiences. And these experiences may be found in the galleries of the future. Preserved. But it's in the poetry where the exhibits actually live. And it's here. Let Seni walk you through the labyrinthine gallery of *Wild Cinnamon and Winter Skin*. '

Lemn Sissay

'Seni Seneviratne poetically weaves a journey from Sri Lanka to Yorkshire. Her poems are lyrical songs with words dancing on the page. This authentic collection leaves you with many scents from the author's past.'

Valerie Mason-John

'Seni Seneviratne's poetry straddles continents and centuries – and does so with an easy fluency. The reader is drawn into her journey of discovery for her 'cinnamon roots' and her exploration of issues of identity and relationships. Personal and universal histories interweave in these poems.'

Debjani Chatterjee

Jeanne Ellin
Who Asks the Caterpillar?
ISBN:1-900715-96-1,pp.104; pub. 2004; price: £8.99

Jeanne Ellin writes consciously as an Anglo-Indian, part of an 'invisible' group that has generally sunk its identity in a general Britishness. She, by contrast, has used her work to explore her sense of Indian origins, but finds her real source of inspiration in the ideas of anomaly and placelessness, themes she explores both directly and obliquely in her poetry. She writes of being 'cell deep... an elephant's child', but also that 'home is a land/ whose texture my feet have forgotten'. But this sense of placelessness also offers the strangers' right 'to a place at every table' and the challenge of living without 'family hand-me-downs', when each day must begin with a naked newness. More obliquely, she uses the mythical figure of the merchild/merechild to explore this sense of inbetweeness; and focuses, in the title poem, on the pleasures and pains of transformation, where after 'a lifetime of voracious consuming' the caterpillar suddenly finds itself as 'an ethereal being' and complains 'I didn't sign up for this spiritual stuff'.

All Peepal Tree titles are available from the website
www.peepaltreepress.com
with a money back guarantee, secure credit card ordering
and fast delivery throughout the world at cost or less.

Peepal Tree Press is celebrated as the home of challenging and inspiring literature from the Caribbean and Black Britain. Visit www.peepaltreepress.com to read sample poems and reviews, discover new authors, established names and access a wealth of information. Subscribe to our mailing list for news of new books and events.

Contact us at:
Peepal Tree Press, 17 King's Avenue, Leeds LS6 1QS, UK
Tel: +44 (0) 113 2451703 E-mail: contact@peepaltreepress.com